# Volcanoes

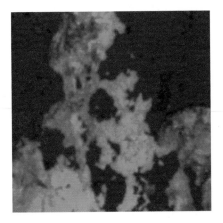

Written by Sarah O'Neil

sundance

# Contents

What Is a Volcano?  4

Inside a Volcano  6

Lava and Ash  8

Active Volcanoes  10

Dormant Volcanoes  11

Extinct Volcanoes  12

Mount St. Helens  14

After an Eruption  16

Where Volcanoes Are Found  18

Index  20

# What Is a Volcano?

The outer layer of the earth is made of cold, hard rock. It is called the crust. Inside the crust, there is very hot, melted rock called magma.

Some parts of the earth's crust are very thin, and the magma can push its way to the surface. When this happens, a volcano is formed.

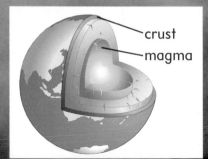

crust
magma

A volcano erupting in Hawaii.

## Inside a Volcano

Volcanoes explode when magma pushes through the earth's crust. This explosion is called an eruption.

During an eruption, magma, steam, poisonous gases, and ash are forced up the vent of the volcano. The magma then flows over the edge of the crater. When magma comes out of a volcano, it is called lava.

crate

vent—an opening in the earth's crust

crust

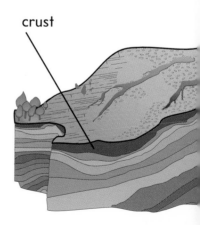

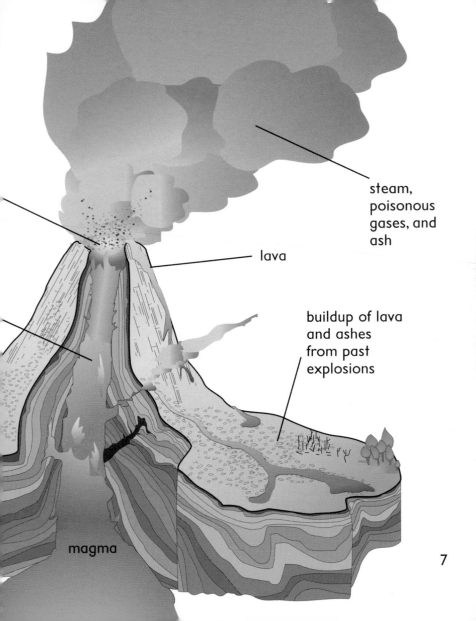

steam,
poisonous
gases, and
ash

lava

buildup of lava
and ashes
from past
explosions

magma

7

Lava is red-hot, liquid rock.

## Lava and Ash

Lava can be thrown into the air, or it can flow down the side of a volcano. Lava is so hot that it melts and burns everything in its path.

The ash that falls from the volcano can cover buildings and trees.

Lava burns everything in its path.

9

# Active Volcanoes

Volcanoes that are likely to erupt are called active. There are more than 800 active volcanoes in the world today.

Cotopaxi is in the Andes in South America. It is the highest active volcano in the world.

## Dormant Volcanoes

Volcanoes that haven't erupted for a long time are called dormant. A dormant volcano might not erupt for years or centuries.

A dormant volcano in Antarctica.

## Extinct Volcanoes

Some volcanoes stop erupting. When a volcano stops erupting, it becomes extinct. An extinct volcano will probably never erupt again.

Lakes sometimes form in the crater of an extinct volcano. The water may come from underground streams or rainfall.

The Glasshouse Mountains in Australia are volcanoes that have been extinct for millions of years.

## Mount St. Helens

In 1980, Mount St. Helens, in Washington state, erupted. It had been dormant for 123 years when it erupted. The eruption lasted for nine hours and blew away the whole side of the mountain. Fifty-seven people were killed. It also caused a lot of damage and pollution.

Mount St. Helens started to smoke before it erupted.

Left:
Mount St. Helens erupting.

Below:
Mount St. Helens after the eruption.

15

## After an Eruption

After a volcano has erupted, nothing lives or grows near it for many years. Eventually dirt blows on to the land that was covered by lava and ash. Seeds are then blown or are dropped by birds on the soil. Soon small plants start to grow.

After a volcano erupts, plants may not grow again for many years.

As more soil builds up, bigger and bigger plants can grow and animals return. After hundreds of years, a forest may have grown all over the extinct volcano. The only sign that a volcano existed may be a large crater or a lake.

Crater Lake National Park, Oregon, where volcanoes once erupted.

## Where Volcanoes Are Found

Volcanoes are usually found near the edges of the thick rock plates that make up the earth's surface. These rock plates are called tectonic plates.

On the edge of the tectonic plates, the crust is thinner. This is where volcanoes are most likely to form. There are often groups of volcanoes along the edges of tectonic plates.

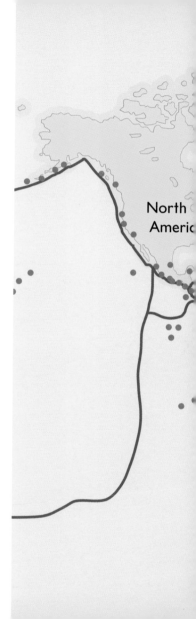

North America

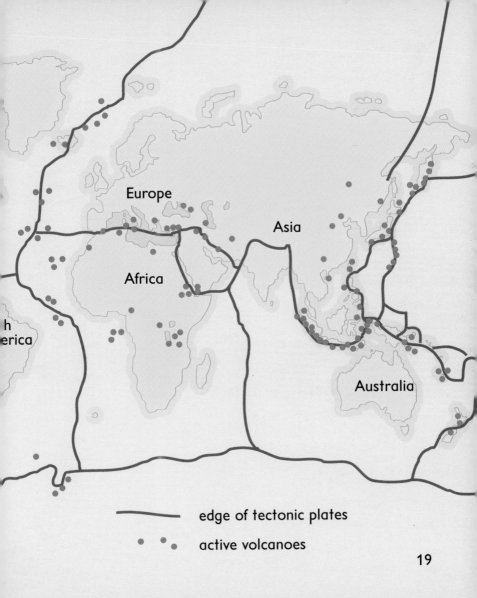

Europe

Asia

Africa

h
erica

Australia

—————  edge of tectonic plates

•  •  •  active volcanoes

19

# Index

active volcanoes  10, 18, 19

ash  6, 7, 8, 16

crater  6, 13, 17

crust  4, 6, 18

dormant volcanoes  11, 14

extinct volcanoes  12, 13, 17

gases  6, 7

lava  6, 7, 8, 9, 16

magma  4, 6, 7

steam  6, 7

tectonic plates  18, 19

vent  6